# HYMN TUNES

## for the
## reluctant organist

Arranged by
JANETTE COOPER

OXFORD UNIVERSITY PRESS
1987

*Oxford University Press, Walton Street, Oxford OX2 6DP*

*Oxford New York Toronto*
*Delhi Bombay Calcutta Madras Karachi*
*Petaling Jaya Singapore Hong Kong Tokyo*
*Nairobi Dar es Salaam Cape Town*
*Melbourne Auckland*

*and associated companies in*
*Beirut Berlin Ibadan Nicosia*

*Oxford is a trade mark of Oxford University Press*

*Published in the United States*
*by Oxford University Press, New York*

*© Oxford University Press 1987*

*Set by Wyvern Typesetting Limited.*
*Printed in Great Britain by*
*Butler and Tanner, Frome, Somerset*

Oxford University Press wishes to thank the owners or controllers of copyright material
for allowing simplified versions to be made of the following tunes:

| Composer | Permission granted by | Tune no. |
| --- | --- | --- |
| Appleford, P. | © 1960 Josef Weinberger Ltd. Reproduced by permission of the copyright owners | 69 |
| Buck, P. C. | Oxford University Press | 48 |
| Carter, S. | © Stainer & Bell Ltd. Reprinted with permission | 134 |
| Dykes Bower, J. | Exors. of the late John Dykes Bower | 67 |
| Fleming, M. (arr.) | The Royal School of Church Music | 107 |
| Greatorex, W. | Oxford University Press | 163 |
| Harwood, B. | Exors. of the late Basil Harwood | 73, 147 |
| Howells, H. | Novello & Co. Ltd. | 82 |
| Ireland, J. | © The John Ireland Trust | 72 |
| Nicholson, S. H. | Hymns Ancient & Modern Ltd. | 15, 27 |
| Routley, E. | Oxford University Press | 136 |
| Rowlands, W. P. | © G. A. Gabe, Swansea, Wales | 14 |
| Shaw, M. F. | Oxford University Press | 24 |
| Shaw, M. F. | William Elkin Music Services, on behalf of J. Curwen & Sons Ltd. | 68, 76 |
| Slater, G. A. | Oxford University Press | 116 |
| Taylor, C. V. | Oxford University Press | 1 |
| Terry, R. R. | Search Press Ltd. | 13 |
| Vaughan Williams, R. | Oxford University Press | 35, 42, 62, 64, 86, 103, 135, 144 |
| Westbrook, F. B. | Oxford University Press | 156 |

# PREFACE

Although hymns are fundamental to the musical content of most church services, experience often shows that for the organist the successful performance of consecutive block harmonies in four parts calls for considerable skill. It is in fact one of the most demanding of keyboard functions, understandably made the more so for those with a limited technique and facility. Janette Cooper, as the architect of the RSCM's successful Reluctant Organist scheme, has an uncanny instinct for what is needed in this particular field. It is therefore hardly surprising that she has responded so successfully in rearranging a wide cross-section of the tunes most commonly in use.

Many who might otherwise feel at a disadvantage will now be able to play hymns with far greater assurance, and project a greater measure of confidence in their accompanying of this important aspect of church services; moreover, they will not need to use the pedals. I hazard a guess that some of the less reluctant will also have cause to be grateful for these arrangements which lie so easily and logically under the fingers.

This book will encourage organists by making their task the easier to grapple with. It should also contribute towards the realization that hymns well-played are an enrichment to the completeness of worship.

LIONEL DAKERS
*Director, Royal School of Church Music*

# INTRODUCTION

Those who tamper with favourite hymns live dangerously. They risk arousing strong passions and may be accused of singlehandedly sending the Church to the dogs. So be it. I have one reason for putting my head on such an uncomfortable block: to ease the lot of the organist who is unable to manage the hymns as printed in the ordinary hymn-book.

At this point, readers will instantaneously split into two categories. The reaction of one group will be, 'Organists who can't even manage hymns? The Church would be better off without them.' This kind of reader should close this book immediately; his blood-pressure will otherwise suffer, and he is probably someone who never knew, or cannot remember, the difficulties of learning hymns experienced by those with little previous musical training.

So the following pages are for the other category—for the Reluctant Organist. If you are one such, you hardly need a definition: you do not need me to remind you that the Vicar press-ganged you into attempting 'just one hymn this evening, because the Organist is ill/dead/gone off in a huff—only tonight, thank you, because by next week we shall be sorted out.' Next week, next month, next year, we are only sorted out to the extent that you are still presiding—you, with your thirty-year-old Grade Two piano certificate, your inability to read more than one note at a time (*Every . . . Good . . . Boy . . .* yes, that note is D), your non-existent repertoire; you, with your mounting weekend panic, yet desire not to let the side down: how are you to learn a minimum of five hymns each week? It is the stuff of which nervous breakdowns are made and on which marriages have foundered.

A good hymn tune is easy to sing but not necessarily easy to play. Ordinary keyboard music is easier in that the bass is often static for a few beats while the top moves, then vice versa. Not so with hymns. Block harmonies change relentlessly on most beats, added to which tenths, so frequently written in the bass staff, cannot be stretched. While you puzzle over a solution, the singers move smartly on and all is lost. Paradoxically, the singers are the greatest problem of all, yet are the sole *raison d'être* of any hymn. To do their job well, they need to be supported by and led with rhythmic, well-shaped organ playing. But how can your playing be this if eyes and fingers just cannot cope with so many notes?

So I have taken some frequently-used hymn tunes and done some pruning. I have mostly cut down four-part harmony to three: one could say that 25% of note-learning is thereby cut! But do not assume that this can be done satisfactorily just by omitting the alto or tenor of any hymn. The middle part has been distributed between the hands in such a way as to eliminate the problem of the tenths. Insecurities can arise when the hands are far apart, so I have kept roughly within the range of two octaves. Keys and harmonies are all consistent with the New Standard Edition of *Hymns Ancient and Modern*: if you play with a choir which is singing standard harmony, you will not part company.

Some fingering is suggested. By starting a passage with a particular finger, it is often possible to play whole bars without shifting hand positions. Two-part chords compound the issue, but the principle remains. My markings are suggestions only: size of hand and individual physical characteristics will sometimes dictate other solutions.

Well-organized fingering will allow legato playing. But bear in mind that 100% legato gives an unshaped and unrhythmic sound, and that to inject silence before certain chords can give a whole line shape and definition which it would otherwise lack. Consider, for instance, the large number of hymns which begin on an upbeat: detach that first chord from its successor and you have shaped the whole phrase. As you do so, keep your fingers in contact with the surface of the keys and you will not get lost.

By definition, the words and music of hymns are inseparable. It is necessary therefore to use this book on the organ desk alongside the book of words—the nearer, the better. At the outset of your enforced career as an organist, new hymns will come thick and fast, probably around four or five each week. Begin on Monday, not Saturday, if you are able, and adopt a set pattern of learning somewhat akin to a sausage machine—it will probably be quicker in the long run. The earlier in this process that words are associated with tunes, the more clearly the identity of the whole hymn will be defined to you; collections will cease to resemble books of identical crossword puzzles. Try a pattern something like this:

1. Read the words to get a general idea of their content.

2. Examine the tune for its key. This will give you a sense of home base and tell you which black notes are needed.

3. Most modern hymn-books use crotchets as the basic unit of pulse, so the majority of tunes have either three or four crotchets in a bar. Decide which before you begin.

4. This book uses commas and double bars to indicate ends of lines. Initially, learn no more than the very last line, and if necessary (as it often is) sort out the left hand first. When you have superimposed the right hand, notice how many times the key chord has recurred: the sense of home base just mentioned will be reinforced.

5. Flick your eyes over to the last line of the words of verse one, back to the line of music just learnt, and sing as you play.

6. Look at the last line of the words of verse two, look at the line of music just learnt, and sing the new words as you play.

7. Run down a few more verses, last lines only.

8. Repeat the process, this time isolating the penultimate line of the tune, then matching it with the penultimate line of each verse.

9. Join these last two lines, with a pause in between to gather your wits. Try these lines in several verses, gradually shortening the pause.

10. Continue to work backwards, until all lines have been learnt singly, joined in pairs, then by fours.

In this way the words will become allied quite painlessly to the tune with no separate process needed. Do not try to memorize either all the tune or all the words—that is a great bore. But most of us can assimilate three or four chords and a rather larger number of words. If the same fingering patterns have been used throughout this repetition, the automatic pilot is more likely to function when Sunday panic arises. It will also take a shorter time to re-learn the tune later in the year, because eyes, ears, *and* fingers will be on vaguely familiar ground.

All this can be carried out at home on a piano, providing that the sustaining pedal is not used. By the time the hymn is transferred to the organ, you will know if it is essentially penitential, joyful, militant, or contemplative in nature: this will help you to select suitable stops.

Aim at all times to make clean, clear sounds, to use the minimum number of stops, and not to be too clever. If there are two manuals, select single 8' and 4' stops on both. Trial and error will show that some of these are large, some small, some strident, some heavy, and one or two plain nasty. If more brightness is needed, add a 2', or try 8' and 2' without the intermediate 4'. Things to avoid are whole bunches of 8' stops, 16' stops on manuals, and anything labelled *Voix Célestes*. Add or subtract not more than one stop between verses, and only do so if it is a well-considered and practised move, firmly pencilled into the copy. The use of stops is discussed in detail in my Reluctant Organist Handbook and Cassette, both published by the Royal School of Church Music.

Gaps between verses should be consistent and rhythmic, and should allow comfortable time for the singers to breathe. Try counting through the last chord of each verse for its full length, then say, 'One, two' in the same pulse and begin the next verse. If you linger on the first chord, the singers will linger longer.

Those who have embarked on pedalling in hymns will probably have no need of this book. Do not try to use your feet and this book together: it will not work. And please do not try to put in 'just a few' pedal notes to give added depth: it will be like going along a road full of potholes.

Only names of tunes have been used here, and they are arranged in alphabetical order. If your particular *bête noire* is not among them, let me know—perhaps another collection can be made. But perhaps by that time the present generation of Reluctant Organists will be far too clever to need that kind of help.

JANETTE COOPER
*Warden, Royal School of Church Music*

# Hymn Tunes
## for the Reluctant Organist

arranged by
Janette Cooper

## 1 Abbot's Leigh 87. 87. D.

Printed in Great Britain

OXFORD UNIVERSITY PRESS, WALTON STREET, OXFORD OX2 6DP

## 2 Abends L.M.

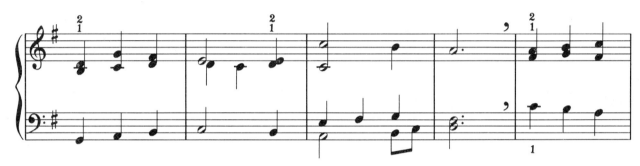

## 3 Abridge C.M.

## 4 Adeste Fideles

## 5 Albano C.M.

## 6 All for Jesus 87. 87.

# 7 All things bright and beautiful 76. 76. and refrain

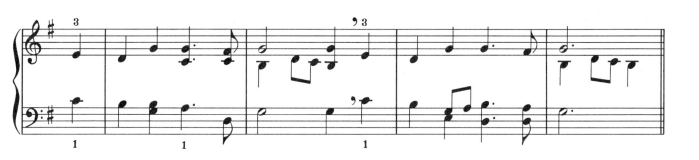

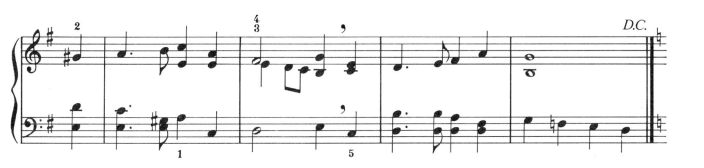

## 8 Angel Voices 85. 85. 843.

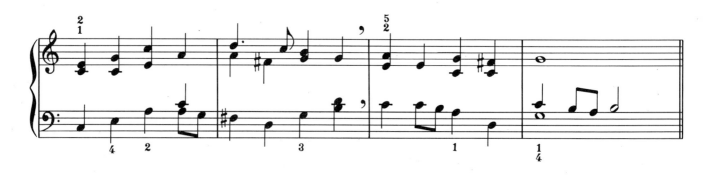

## 9 Aurelia 76. 76. D.

10 Aus der Tiefe 77.77.

## 11 Austria 87. 87. D.

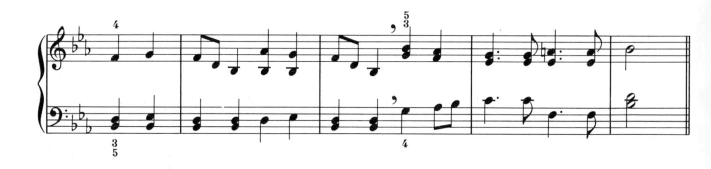

## 12 Beulah C.M.

## 13 Billing C.M.

## 14 Blaenwern 87. 87. D.

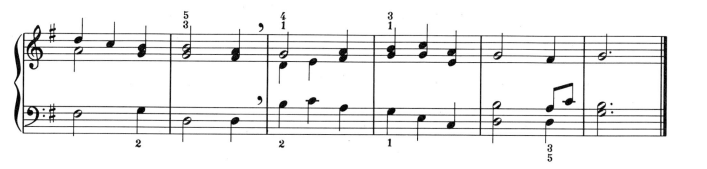

## 15 Bow Brickhill L.M.

## 16 Bread of Heaven 77.77.77.

## 17 Breslau L.M.

## 18 Bristol C.M.

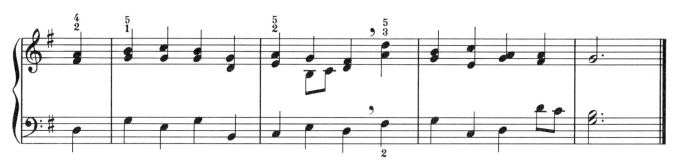

## 19 Buckland 77.77.

## 20 Capetown 77. 75.

## 21 Carlisle S.M.

## 22 Caswall 65. 65.

## 23 Christe Sanctorum 11 11. 11 5.

## 24 Crediton C.M.

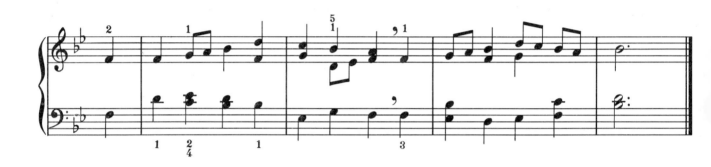

## 25 Crimond C.M.

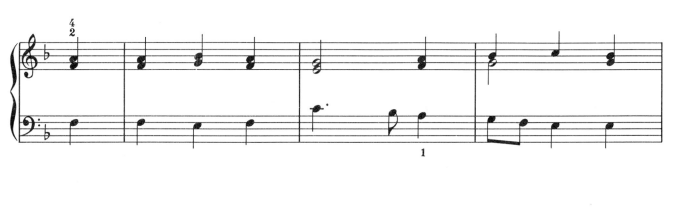

## 26 Cross of Jesus 87.87.

## 27 Crucifer 10 10. and refrain

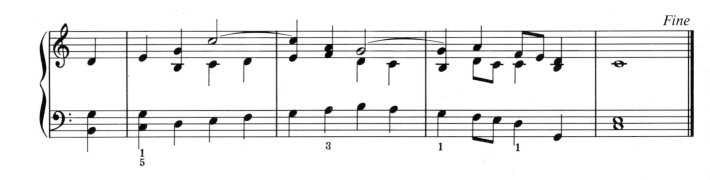

## 28 Crucis victoria C.M.

## 29 Cwm Rhondda 87. 87. 47.

## 30 Darwall's 148th 66. 66. 44. 44.

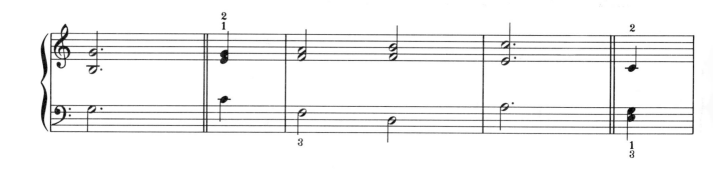

## 31 Deus tuorum militum (Grenoble) L.M.

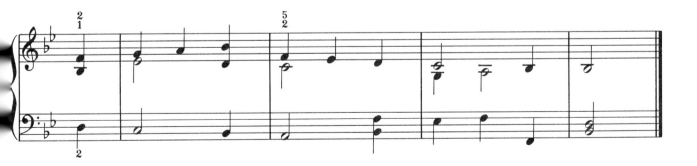

## 32 Diademata D.S.M.

## 33 Dix 77.77.77.

\* The first line of music may be repeated and the second line omitted, if preferred.

## 34 Dominus regit me 87. 87.

## 35 Down Ampney 66. 11. D.

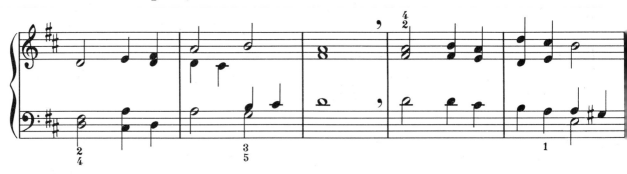

## 36 Duke Street L.M.

## 37 Dundee C.M.

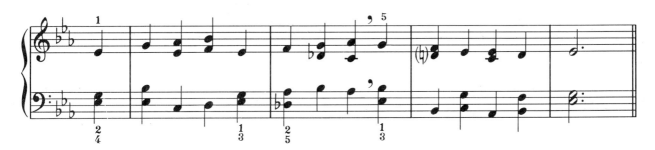

## 38 Easter Hymn 74. 74. D.

## 39 Ellacombe 76. 76. D.

## 40 Evelyns 65. 65. D.

## 41 Eventide 10 10. 10 10

## 42 Forest Green  D.C.M. Words irreg.

## 43 Franconia S.M.

## 44 Fulda L.M.

## 45 Galilee L.M.

## 46 Gelobet sei Gott (Vulpius) 888. and Alleluyas

47 Gerontius C.M.

## 48 Gonfalon Royal L.M.

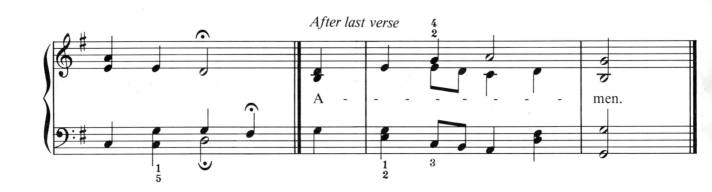

## 49 Gopsal 66. 66. 88.

* E is the original note written by Handel, but many hymnbooks show an F here.

## 50 Gwalchmai 7 4. 7 4. D.

## 51 Halton Holgate 87. 87.

## 52 Hanover 55. 55. 65. 65.

## 53 Heathlands 77. 77. 77.

## 54 Helmsley 87. 87. 47.

## 55 Hereford L.M.

## 56 Hollingside 77. 77. D.

57 Horsley C.M.

## 58 Hyfrydol 87. 87. D.

## 59 Irby 87. 87. 77.

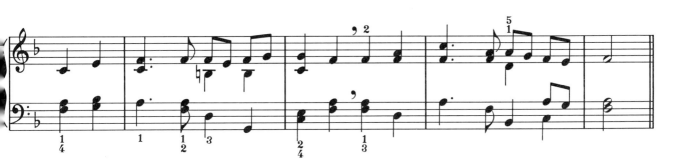

## 60 Irish C.M.

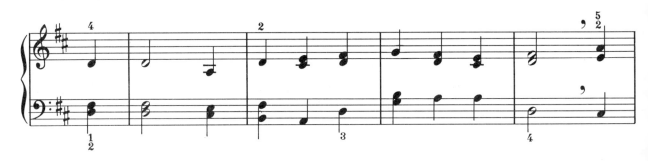

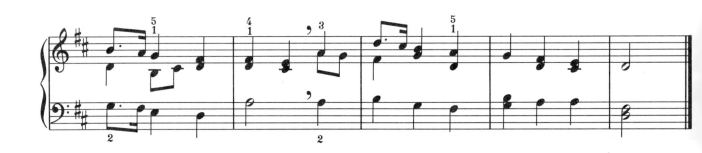

## 61 Jerusalem D.L.M.

## 62 Kingsfold D.C.M.

## 63 Kocher (Knecht) 76. 76.

## 64 Lasst uns erfreuen 88. 44. 88. and Alleluyas

## 65 Laudate Dominum 10 10. 11 11.

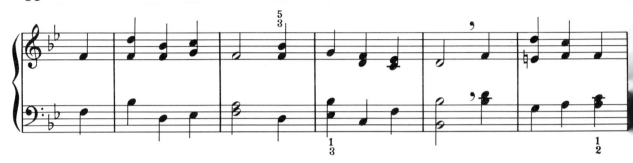

## 66 Laus Deo (Redhead No. 46) 87. 87.

## 67 Let us break bread

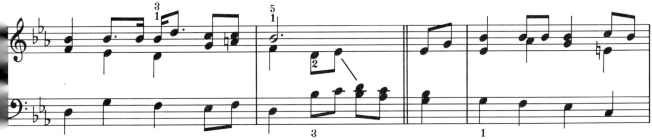

## 68 Little Cornard 66.66.88.

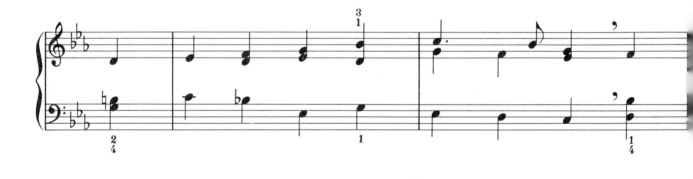

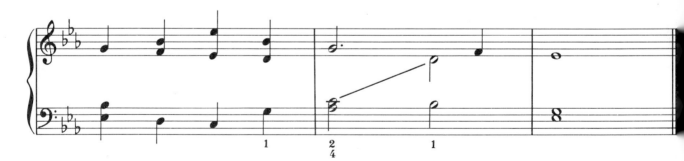

## 69 Living Lord

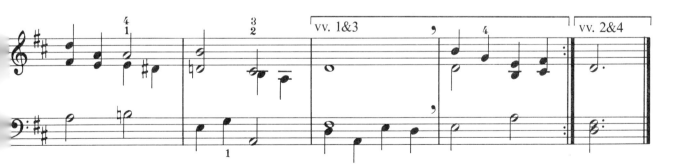

## 70 Lobe den Herren (Hast du denn, Jesu) 14 14. 4. 7. 8.

## 71 Love Divine 87. 87.

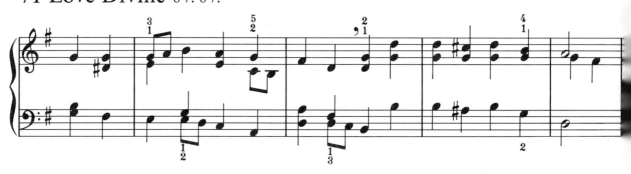

## 72 Love Unknown 66. 66. 44. 44.

## 73 Luckington 10 4. 6 6. 6 6. 10 4.

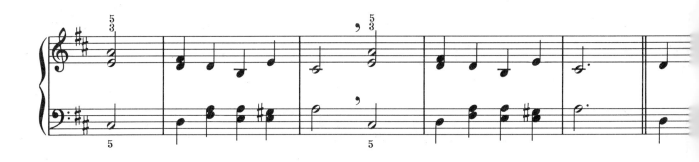

## 74 Maccabaeus 10 11. 11 11. and refrain

## 75 Mannheim 87. 87. 87.

## 76 Marching 87. 87.

## 77 Martyrdom C.M.

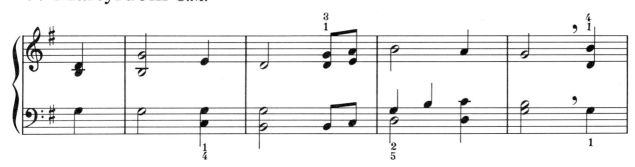

## 78 Melcombe L.M.

## 79 Melita 88. 88. 88.

## 80 Mendelssohn 7777.7777.77.

## 81 Merton 87. 87.

## 82 Michael 87. 87. 3 3. 7.

## 83 Miles Lane C.M.

## 84 Misericordia 8 8. 8. 6.

## 85 Monkland 77. 77.

86 Monks Gate 11 11. 12 11.

## 87 Morning Hymn L.M.

## 88 Moscow 664. 666. 4.

## 89 Narenza S.M.

## 90 National Anthem 664.6664.

## 91 Nativity C.M.

## 92 Neander 87.87.87.

## 93 Nicaea 11 12. 12 10.

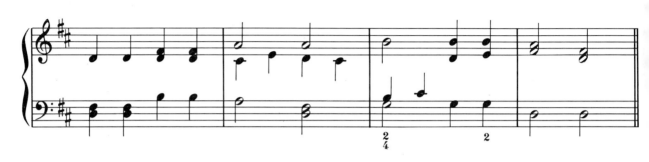

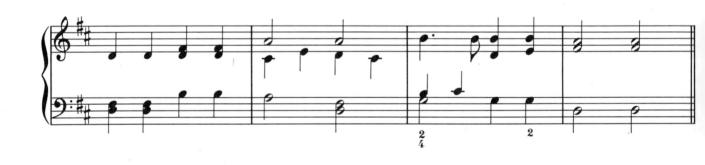

## 94 Noel D.C.M.

## 95 Nun danket 67. 67. 66. 66.

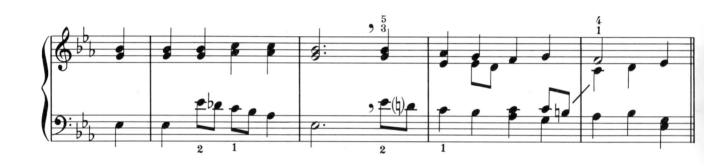

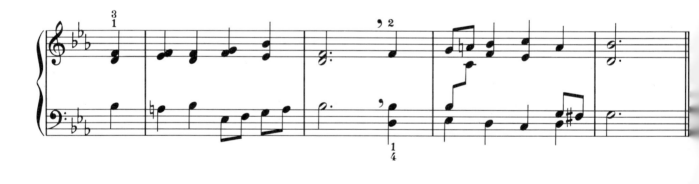

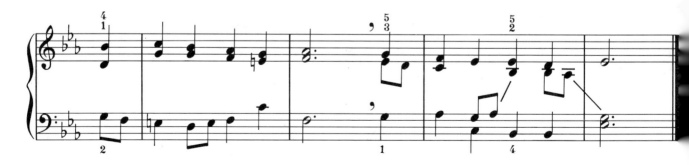

## 96 Old 100<sup>th</sup> L.M.

## 97 Passion Chorale 76. 76. D.

## 98 Pastor pastorum 65. 65.

## 99 Petra (Redhead No. 76) 77. 77. 77.

## 100 Picardy 87. 87. 87.

## 101 Praise, my soul 87. 87. 87.

## 102 Quam Dilecta 66. 66.

## 103 Quem pastores 88. 87.

## 104 Ratisbon 77. 77. 77.

## 105 Ravenshaw 66. 66.

## 106 Regent Square 87. 87. 87.

## 107 Repton 86. 886.

arranged by Michael Fleming

## 108 Rhuddlan 87. 87. 87.

## 109 Richmond C.M.

110 Rockingham L.M.

## 111 Saffron Walden 88. 86.

## 112 St Albinus 78. 784.

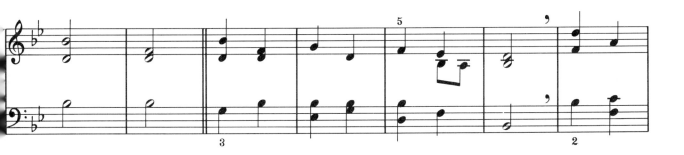

## 113 St Alphege 76. 76.

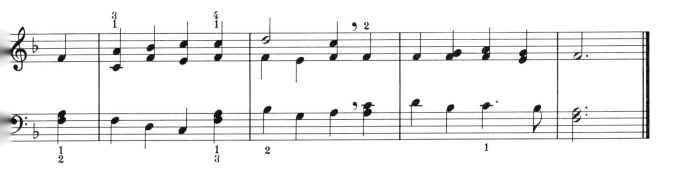

## 114 St Anne C.M.

## 115 St Bernard C.M.

## 116 St Botolph C.M.

## 117 St Cecilia 66. 66.

## 118 St Clement 98. 98.

## 119 St Cuthbert 86. 84.

## 120 St Denio (Joanna) 11. 11. 11. 11.

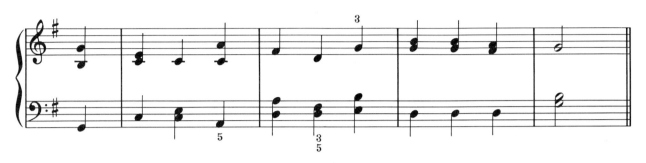

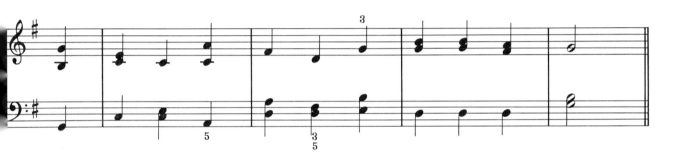

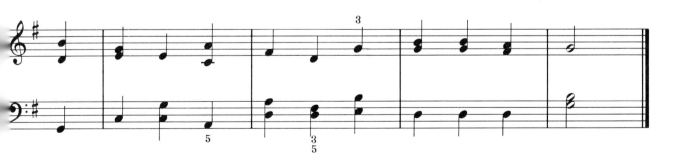

## 121 St Ethelwald S.M.

## 122 St Flavian C.M.

## 123 St Fulbert C.M.

*After last verse*

Al - le - lu - ia.    A - men.

* ♩ in last verse

## 124 St George 77. 77. D.

## 125 St Gertrude 65. 65. *Ter.*

## 126 St Helen 87. 87. 87.

## 127 St Magnus C.M.

## 128 St Oswald 87.87.

## 129 St Peter C.M.

## 130 St Theodulph 76. 76. D.

## 131 St Timothy C.M.

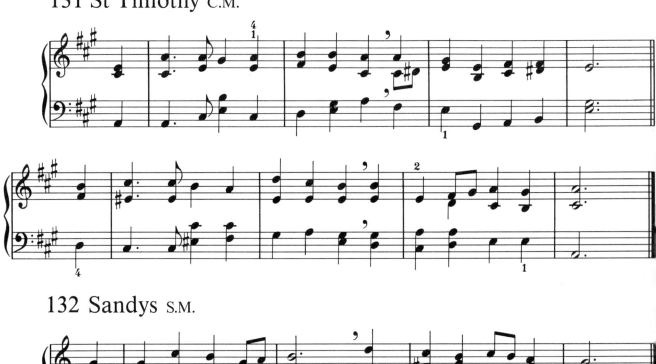

## 132 Sandys S.M.

## 133 Savannah 77.77.

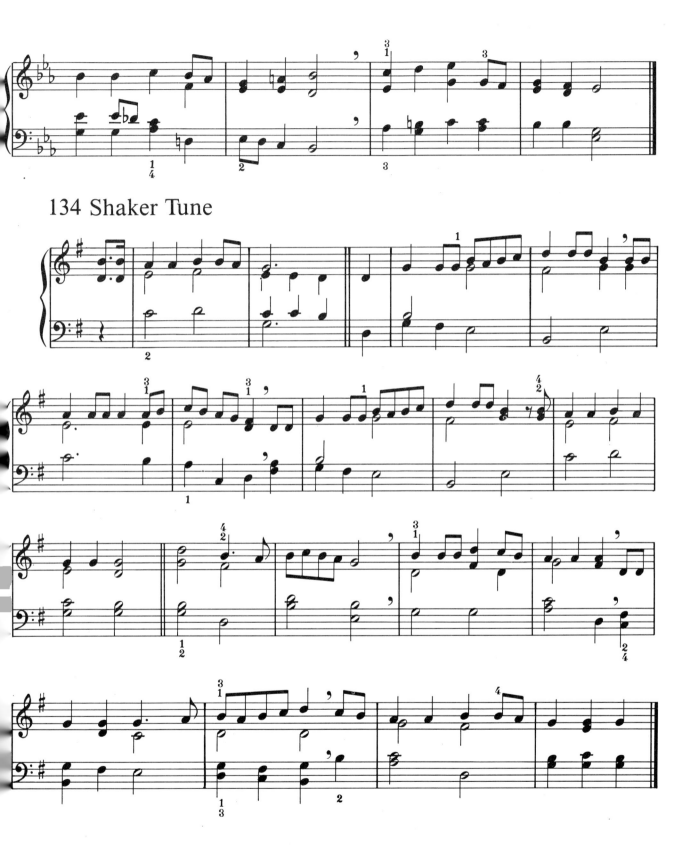

134 Shaker Tune

## 135 Sine Nomine 10 10. 10 4.

## 136 Slane 10 11. 11. 11

## 137 Solothurn L.M.

## 138 Song 1 10 10. 10 10. 10 10.

## 139 Song 34 (Angel's Song) L.M.

## 140 Stockton C.M.

## 141 Strength and Stay 11 10. 11 10.

## 142 Stuttgart 8 7. 8 7.

## 143 Surrey 88.88.88.

## 144 Sussex 87.87.

## 145 Tallis's Canon L.M.

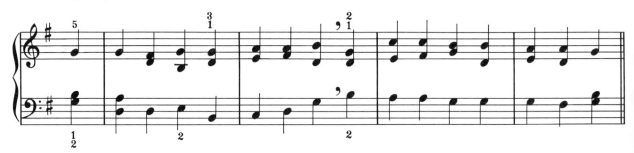

## 146 Tallis's Ordinal C.M.

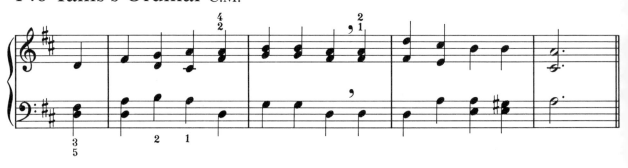

## 147 Thornbury 76. 76. D.

**148 Truro** L.M.

**149 University** C.M.

## 150 University College 77.77.

## 151 Veni Emmanuel 88.88.88.

## 152 Veni Sancte Spiritus 777. D.

## 153 Victory 88. 84.

## 154 Vienna 77.77.

## 155 Wareham L.M.

## 156 Were you there? 10 10. and refrain

## 157 Westminster C.M.

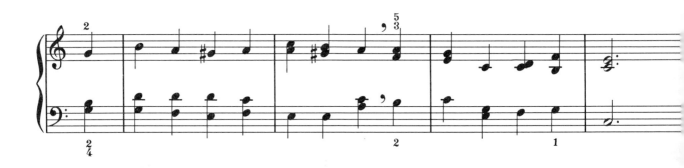

## 158 Westminster Abbey 87. 87. 87.

**159 Wiltshire** C.M.

## 160 Winchester New L.M.

## 161 Winchester Old C.M.

## 162 Wir pflügen  76. 76. 76. 76. 66. 84.

## 163 Woodlands 10 10. 10 10.

## 164 Württemburg 77. 77. 4.

## 165 Yorkshire 10 10. 10 10. 10 10.

# INDEX